MONROE TOWNSH

MONSTER JOKES

compiled by Diane Dow Suire
illustrated by Llyn Hunter

created by The Child's World

 CHILDRENS PRESS, CHICAGO

Cover art by Diana L. Magnuson

Library of Congress Cataloging in Publication Data

Suire, Diane Dow.
    Monster jokes / compiled by Diane Dow Suire ; illustrated by Llyn
Hunter ; created by The Child's World.
      p. cm.
      Summary: Presents an illustrated collection of jokes, knock
-knocks, and riddles about Frankenstein, Godzilla, King Kong,
Dracula, vampires, werewolves, and other monsters.
      ISBN 0-516-01866-3
      1. Monsters—Juvenile humor.   2. Wit and humor, Juvenile.
3. Riddles, Juvenile.   [1. Monsters—Wit and humor.   2. Jokes.
3. Riddles.]   I. Hunter, Llyn, ill.   II. Child's World (Firm)
III. Title.
PN6231.M665S95   1988   88-17487
818'.5402—dc19   CIP
                                                                  AC

1 2 3 4 5 6 7 8 9 10 11 12 R 95 94 93 92 91 90 89 88

TABLE OF CONTENTS

Ghoulish Godzilla 4

Funnysteins 8
    (Frankenstein Jokes)

Dracula and Other Vampires 12

Weird Werewolves 20

King Kong 24

Bigfoot 28

Loch Ness and Other Sea Monsters 32

Still More Monsters 36

Ghoulish
Godzilla

Why does Godzilla wag his tail?
Because no one else will wag it for him.

Why did Godzilla scream when the tailor pressed his pants?
Because he was still in them.

Why does Godzilla have a pointed tail?
From standing too close to the pencil sharpener.

What happened when Godzilla lost his tail?
He went to the re-tail shop.

Why does Godzilla have wrinkled legs?
From tying his tennis shoes too tight.

What do you call a sea monster who works in Godzilla's store?
A scalesman.

What do you call a giant dentist with scaly skin and a long tail?
An orthodonzilla.

Why does Godzilla take cold medicine?
To quiet his coffin.

What's Godzilla's favorite bean?
A human bean.

Why does Godzilla eat with his tail?
He can't take it off.

How far can Godzilla walk into a park?
Halfway. After that he will be walking out.

How does Godzilla get into locked cemeteries?
With skeleton keys.

What do you call the man who takes on Godzilla?
Stupid.

How does Godzilla dance?
Very loudly.

Teacher: What is yellow, has wheels, and lies on
its back?
Godzilla: A dead school bus.

When can Godzilla, Bigfoot, Frankenstein, and
Dracula go out under one little umbrella and not
get wet?
When it is not raining.

Funnysteins

What has. . .

two legs like Frankenstein,

two eyes like Frankenstein,

two hands like Frankenstein,

and looks like Frankenstein,

but is not Frankenstein?

A picture of Frankenstein.

What has six feet and two hands?
Frankenstein and his dog.

What kind of tie did Frankenstein wear to the formal party?
A boo-tie.

Why did Frankenstein take a bath before breaking out of jail?
To make a clean getaway.

What invention allowed Frankenstein to walk
through walls?
  A door.

Why did Frankenstein go over the hill?
  Because he couldn't go under it.

Why did Frankenstein put a saddle on the horse
backwards?
  He wanted to see where he had been.

Who does Frankenstein write letters to?
His best fiend.

Why did Frankenstein give up boxing?
He didn't want to ruin his looks.

What are Frankenstein's favorite flowers?
Mari-ghouls and bleeding hearts.

What does Frankenstein call a dungeon?
The family room.

How did Frankenstein decorate for his party?
With creep paper and balloons.

What's the best way to call Frankenstein?
Long distance.

What is the best way to get something out from under Frankenstein?
Wait for him to move.

Dracula and Other Vampires

What kind of pants did Dracula wear to the square dance?
Designer boo-jeans.

What should you do when you see Dracula?
Hope Dracula does not see you.

What does Dracula drink while watching softball?
Ghoul-aid.

How do you keep Dracula from biting his nails?
Give him some necks.

What did the little girl say when she saw
Dracula wearing sunglasses?
Nothing. She didn't recognize him.

What kind of bars can't keep Dracula in jail?
Candy bars.

What did Dracula's cousin do on the baseball
team?
He was the bat boy.

What does Dracula put on before he goes
swimming?
A water-proof cape.

What's Dracula's favorite dessert?
Boo-berry pie.

What's Dracula's favorite painting?
The Moan-a Lisa.

When does Dracula have breakfast?
In the moaning.

Does Dracula really do all the awful things you
see in the movies?
Sometimes he uses stuntmen.

What was the first thing that wore out on
Dracula's car?
The spook plugs.

How did Dracula keep mosquitoes out of his
haunted house?
He put up scream windows.

What does Dracula eat for breakfast?
Shrouded wheat.

Why did Dracula think spanking was good for his
son's education?
It made him smart.

Why did the captain ask Dracula to leave the
submarine?
Dracula liked to sleep with the windows open.

What is the best thing to do if you find a vampire
in your bed?
Sleep somewhere else.

What does a vampire like to do for a good time?
Go to the club and boogie.

Where does a vampire go for a holiday?
Mali-boo.

Suzie Vampire: What happened to the man who sat in the purple and red paint?
Silly Vampire: He came to a violet end.

Sammy Vampire: What are you always sure of finding when you reach into the pocket of a vampire?
Suzie Vampire: Your hand.

Why did the vampire go on a diet?
She wanted to keep her ghoulish figure.

Where will the lady vampire be when the lights go out?
In the dark.

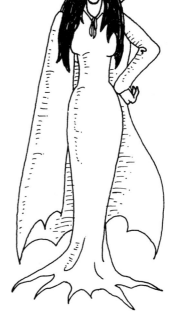

How does a vampire flirt?
She bats her eyes.

Why did the vampire go to the dentist?
To improve his bite.

What did the vampire do when he lost his head?
  Employed a head hunter.

Who does a vampire get letters from?
  His fang club.

What happened to the tomatoes the vampire
planted?
  They grue-some.

Why did the vampire swing through the trees?
  *He didn't want to get his new shoes dirty
  walking.*

What comes out at night and goes:
flap, flap, chomp, ouch?
  A vampire with a large cavity.

What happened to the vampire who covered
himself with vanishing cream?
  Nobody knows.

Why is it so hard to borrow money from midget
vampires?
  They're always short themselves.

Vampire 1: What loses its head every morning,
but gets it back at night?
Vampire 2: A pillow.

Weird Werewolves

What is hairy, has fangs, and lives at the North Pole?
A lost werewolf.

What do werewolves have that no other monsters have?
Baby werewolves.

When is a werewolf not a werewolf?
When he turns into a store.

What do werewolves eat for lunch?
Boo-loney sandwiches.

What do you get when you cross a werewolf and a rooster?

An animal that howls when the sun rises.

What has fangs and is hairy and blue all over?

A werewolf at the North Pole.

What language do werewolves speak?

Werewolveese.

In a werewolf cemetery, how many werewolves are buried?

All of them.

Why do werewolves make good football players?

Because they always reach the ghoul line.

What did the werewolf say when he looked in the mirror?
   "Terror, terror on the wall...."

Why did the werewolf take up tennis?
   He wanted to raise a racquet.

Why does the werewolf have so much hair?
   Because he doesn't have the money for a haircut.

Why is the werewolf like a set of false teeth?
   They both come out at night.

Why did the werewolf have a stomachache?
He wolfed down his meal.

What do you give a werewolf with a cold?
A claw-kerchief.

How did the werewolf make a mothball?
He hit him with a fly swatter.

If you cross an anteater with a werewolf, what
will you have?
An ant shortage.

King Kong

What is hairy and blue and very big?
King Kong, holding his breath.

How do you talk to King Kong?
Use big words.

What do you call King Kong's baby who weighs in at 420 pounds?
Slim.

How many bananas can King Kong eat on an empty stomach?
One. After eating one banana, his stomach isn't empty.

Why does King Kong like peanuts?
Because he thinks it's an easy comic strip to read.

Why did the Cyclops like to play with King Kong?
Because he was tons of fun.

How can you tell when King Kong's been in your kitchen?
By the peanut shells left on the table.

What did King Kong find to be the hardest thing about learning to ride a bicycle?
The thing he fell on.

What do you call a 3,000 pound gorilla?
"*Sir.*"

What do you give King Kong in an ice cream shop?
Anything he wants.

What allergy does King Kong have?
Who knows, but I'm sure I don't want to be around when he sneezes!

How do you tell a sea monster from King Kong?
The sea monster is the one that doesn't look like King Kong.

What time is it when King Kong sits on a fence?
Time to get a new fence.

What do you get if you cross King Kong and a parakeet?
A messy cage.

How can you prevent King Kong from charging?
Take away his credit card.

What might you find between King Kong's toes?
Slow running natives.

How do you make a sandwich for King Kong?
First you get a giant loaf of bread . . . .

Bigfoot

What was the best thing Bigfoot put into a pie?
His teeth.

What would you do if Bigfoot sat in front of you
at the movies?
Miss a lot of the movie.

Why does Bigfoot eat less than Count Dracula?
Because he makes a little go a long way.

Why did Bigfoot cross the road?
To get to the other side.

What bird can't fly as high as Bigfoot can jump?
A bird in a cage.

How did Bigfoot drop a full glass and spill no water?
The glass he dropped was full of milk.

When is Bigfoot like a little boy's suit?
When his tongue has a coat and his breath comes in short pants.

What happened when the canary flew into Bigfoot?
Shredded tweet.

What do you call Bigfoot when he has cotton in his ears?
Anything you wish. He can't hear you.

Why does Bigfoot like the fall?
It's the haunting season.

What do you call a monster who wears a size 20 shoe?
BIGFOOT.

How can you tell if Bigfoot has been in your refrigerator?
By the footprints in the jello.

What do you get if you cross a snail and Bigfoot?
The world's slowest monster.

What would you get if you crossed Bigfoot with a chicken?
The biggest cluck around.

What kind of letters does Bigfoot like to read in hot weather?

Fan mail.

Bigfoot: Teacher, why did the two-headed monster receive a higher grade than I?
Teacher: Two heads are better than one.

Bigfoot: What was my name in first grade?
Teacher: Bigfoot.
Bigfoot: What was my name in second grade?
Teacher: Bigfoot.
Bigfoot: Knock-knock.
Teacher: Who's there?
Bigfoot: Don't tell me you've already forgotten me!

Loch Ness and Other Sea Monsters

Why didn't the Loch Ness Monster want to play with his friends?

He was a stick-in-the-mud.

What do you get if you cross an ocean with a monster?

Wet.

What do you call a sea monster who's late for school?

An overslept-ile.

What does the sea monster do when he's happy?

Claps his hands — all eight of them.

What does a sea monster say when she has a lot
of homework?
  I'm swamped.

What is the difference between a peanut-butter
sandwich and the Loch Ness Monster?
  *The Loch Ness Monster doesn't stick to the roof
of your mouth.*

What is blue and slimy and has one hundred legs?
  I don't know, but it's crawling into your boat.

When a sea monster falls into the water, what's
the first thing he does?
  Gets wet.

Sea Monster: Do you have any alligator shoes?
Shoe Salesman: Sure. What size does your alligator wear?

Willy: Where do sea monsters sleep?
Silly: In water beds.

Willy: Where do sea monsters wash?
Silly: In river basins.

Zoologist: There is a 10-foot water snake in this tank.
Student: You can't fool me. Snakes don't have feet.

Loch Ness Monster: Why do you have alphabet soup every day?
Little Boy: So I can eat and practice reading at the same time.

What is slimy and wet and teaches school?
The teacher from the black lagoon.

Sea Teacher: There is a theory that fish is brain food.
Sea Monster: Yes, teacher. I eat it every day.
Sea Teacher: Oh, well, so much for that theory!

Sea Monster I: That crust on the salmon cake was tough.
Sea Monster II: That wasn't the crust. That was the paper plate.

Teacher: Why is the Mississippi such an unusual river?
River Rat: Because it has four eyes and can't see.

Teacher: What can you tell us about the Dead Sea?
Sea Monster: I didn't even know it was sick.

Still More Monsters

What instrument did the lighthouse monster
play?
The fog horn.

Why did the Invisible Man quit the game?
Because he didn't have a ghost of a chance.

What does the Invisible Man drink with cookies?
Evaporated milk.

What looks like the Invisible Man?
The Invisible Man's twin brother.

Who is the thirstiest monster in the world?
The one who drank Canada Dry.

How does a monster count to 14?
On his fingers.

What do you do with a blue monster?
Cheer him up.

What did the ghoul call his date?
His ghoul friend.

What game did Dr. Jekyll like most?
Hyde and Seek.

What do spooks like at the fun park?
The roller ghoster.

Bug-eyed Monster 1: Why are you crying?
Bug-eyed Monster 2: My new shoes hurt.
Bug-eyed Monster 1: You've got them on the
wrong feet.

Why is Hodag holding a mirror when his eyes are
closed?
*He wants to see what he looks like when he's
asleep.*

Little Monster: Mother, I hate my teacher.
Mother Monster: Then just eat your salad,
honey.

What is a monster's favorite ball game?
A double-header.

How many huge monsters are born each year?
None! Only baby monsters are born.

Where does a Giant Sphinx sit?
Anywhere he wants to!

Why does the monster cook always put on a high hat?
To cover his head.

How does a ghost eat?
By goblin'.

Who makes up the Monster PTA?
Mummies and deadies.

How is an escaping monster like an airplane pilot?
They both want safe flights.

What does an 800-pound monster say to the lion?
"Here kitty, kitty."

Why did the baby monster put ice in his father's bed?
Because he liked cold pop.

Teacher: If there were nine cats in a boat, and one jumped into the sea, how many would be left?

Sea Monster: None, because they are all copycats.

What monster has eyes that can-
not see and legs that cannot
move, but can jump as high as the
Empire State Building?
*A mummy monster. The Empire
State Building can't jump.*

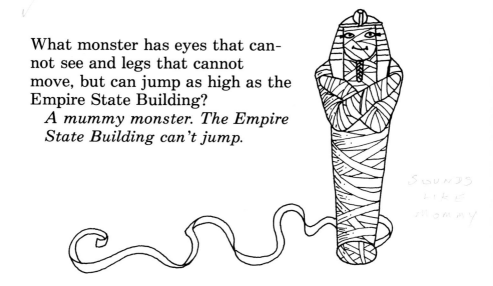

SOUNDS
LIKE
MOMMY

What did the little ghost say to the bully ghost?
"Leave me alone or I'll tell my mummy."

Is it true that the Sphinx will not hurt you if you
carry a slingshot?
That depends on how fast you carry it.

What is the study of monsters called?
Boology.

What did the teacher say to the class of
monsters?
"Hello, boys and ghouls."

Why couldn't the mummy attend the party?
He was tied up at the time.

Why doesn't a mummy ever take a holiday?
He might relax and unwind.

If you saw eight flying monsters with green socks
and one flying monster with red socks, what
would this prove?
*That eight out of nine flying monsters are
wearing green socks.*

How do you make a monster light?
Stick his tail in a socket.

Why did the monster sit on the cinnamon stick?
To keep from falling in the hot cider.

What do you call a monster you shoot out of a
cannon?
Monmunition.

What do you call it when a group of monsters
jumps out at you?
A monbush!

What do you call an
eskimo monster's house?
A monloo.

What is red and white on the outside and scary on
the inside?
Campbell's Cream of Monster Soup.

How do you make a monster float?
*Three scoops of ice cream, some soda, and
one monster.*

Why did the one-eyed sea monster leave his school?
He only had one pupil.

Little Monster: Mother, we played softball
in school today, and I stole third
base.
Mother Monster: Well, you had better take it
right back!

Little Monster: My father beats me up each morning.
Teacher Monster: How awful!
Little Monster: It's not too bad. He gets up at 6 and I get up at 7.

Daddy Monster: What kind of marks did you get in gym class?
Little Monster: I didn't get any marks, only a few bruises.

Monster Librarian: Why are you running through the library?
Little Monster: I'm running to stop a fight.
Monster Librarian: Between whom?
Little Monster: Between me and the guy who's chasing me!

How do you start a monster?
Turn on his monnition.

What's scary and bumps into submarines?
A monster scuba diver.

If you were walking in the woods and saw a
monster, what time would it be?
Time to hide.

What unusual vegetable did the monster find at
the picnic?
A beetnik.

What did the monster find to be the hardest
things to walk in?
Slippers.

Why didn't the flying monsters sing?
They didn't want to be mistaken for birds.

Why did Dracula hit his finger with a hammer?
He wanted to be a swell guy.

What do you get when you cross a monster with an owl?
A creature that scares people but doesn't give a hoot.

What do you get when you cross a monster with a cat?
A town without dogs.

What has one wheel and is frightening?
A monster riding a unicycle.

What happened to the monster who broke her toe?
She gave up ballet dancing.

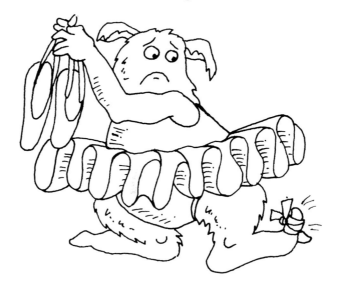

When a monster gets old, what does it wear?
Out.

What's worse than seeing a monster on a dark night?
Seeing its tonsils.

Why don't monsters laugh more often?
With all these awful monster jokes going around, how could they?

j818   Suire, Diane Dow,
SUI   1954-

        Monster jokes   9₆

        $10.60   h   g

DATE		
JUL 3 1989		
JUL 3 1 1989		
SEP 2 9 1989		
NOV 2 9 1989		
MAY 0 5 1990		
AUG 2 7 1990		